IN THIS FOREST OF MONKS

by

Daniel Skach-Mills

IN THIS FOREST OF MONKS

by Daniel Skach-Mills

Copyright © 2012 by Daniel Skach-Mills
skachmills@gmail.com
Designed by Dan Lucas
Author photograph by Scott Steele

ISBN 978-0-615-63836-2

ACKNOWLEDGMENTS

I am grateful to editors of publications where these poems first appeared, perhaps in slightly different versions, or are forthcoming:

Bellowing Ark: "Garnishmint."

Open Spaces: "Ivy."

Sojourners: "A Christmas Candling" "Hiking The Hill That Overlooks The Trappist Abbey Prior To First Vespers Of Christmas, 1990."

Sufi Journal: "Why Monks Choose Silence."

Verseweavers—The Oregon State Poetry Association Poetry Contest Chapbook: "The Monk Who Bakes Bread."

The Westminster Review: "Out Of The Trunk."

Windfall – A Journal of Poetry of Place: "Icon" "Walking Before Compline."

The Windless Orchard: "Herons."

"The Monk Who Bakes Bread" was awarded first place in the fall 2006 *Oregon State Poetry Association "Member's Only"* contest, judged by Laton Carter.

"Out Of The Trunk" was awarded first place in *The Mildred Prather Henderson* national poetry competition, Westminster College (1991). Judge: Sandra Agricola. It was later anthologized in *Prayers To Protest: Poems That Center And Bless Us* (Pudding House, 1998); and in *Urgent Care For The World: Beyond The Waiting Room—An Anthology Of Poems* (Pudding House, 2004).

The epigraph poem which begins, "Being is like a forest …" first appeared in *The Tao of Now*, (Ken Arnold Books, 2008).

The following poems first appeared in *The Hut Beneath The Pine: Tea Poems* (Daniel Skach-Mills, 2011): "On Retreat" "Watching An Old Trappist Drink Tea" (first appeared under the title: "Watching An Old Monk Drink Tea") and "Synesthesia".

"A Forest's Theory Of Human Evolution" was published as a broadside for *The Milwaukie Poetry Series* (2011).

"Manzou" was published as a broadside for *Steeped In Words: The Lan Su Chinese Garden Tea And Poetry Series* (2011).

Portions of the introduction first appeared in *The Friends of William Stafford* newsletter.

"A Christmas Candling" was set to music by Ken Skach-Mills, and performed by *Satori Men's Chorus: Men Singing Peace*.

I would like to thank Dan Lucas, designer and illustrator extraordinaire, whose cover design and layout resonate so beautifully with the spirit of the poems and the place.

I am also grateful for Red Pine's translation of Han Shan's poetry: *The Collected Songs of Cold Mountain*; and Helen Waddell's, *The Desert Fathers*.

And with gratitude to those who were there for me in May, 1992, especially my parents, and Paul and Jeanie.

For Ken

And for all those who have realized
that silence isn't saying anything
the trees don't already know.

Out of the silent forest … where neither hut nor shanty stood, you fashioned their listening into a temple to house their ineffable longing.

— *Rainer Maria Rilke*
Sonnets to Orpheus, 1/1

CONTENTS

Being is like a forest.
It has no need of doorways
because it is its own portal.
It allows entry anywhere
without opening a single latch.

Wherever you walk
the deep roots are there,
but you cannot see them.

Getting lost in these trees
means the end of circling
around and around
what you've always been.

— *Daniel Skach-Mills*

INTRODUCTION

It's March, 1990. And, after three years in monastic formation, I'm taking my first vows as a Trappist monk. As is traditional, I'm standing in the church facing the abbot who is seated in front of the altar. The monastic community is gathered on either side. I have written my vows in my own hand—vows of stability, obedience, and conversion of manners (which includes poverty and chastity)—and am waiting for him to address me with a short talk.

I have no idea what he is going to say. The past year has not been easy. The monastic honeymoon is over, and I have started to question him on how decisions impacting the community are being made. I have become increasingly aware of cracks in the life that—armed with my spackle bucket of 33 year-old idealistic zeal—I am trying to fix rather than accept. I am creative, artistic, and—as the abbot and others in the community know—a poet.

And so, when he looks straight at me and declares that the monastic life is prose, not poetry, I can already hear the death knell of my religious life ringing in his words. Unbidden, and in silent response, the words of an author whose name I can't remember run through my head: "God deals strictly in poetry. Man turns it into prose."

The abbot expelled me from the community in 1992. But in spite of this (or perhaps because of it) I have been struck throughout the years by parallels between the monastic and poetic life which, at first glance, may not be apparent. For example, Oregon's late poet laureate, William Stafford, kept a daily vigil of rising at 4 AM in order to listen and wait for the light of poetic inspiration to appear out of the darkness. The monastic Office of Vigils, held before dawn, is carried out in a similar spirit.

This spirit of listening and waiting, so characteristic of both the monk's and the poet's vocation, is hinted at in the following story from the Christian Desert Fathers:

A young monk asked an elder: "What does it mean to be a monk?"

Pausing briefly, the old monk quietly responded, "To wake up every day asking yourself that question."

Similarly, I can imagine asking William Stafford, "What does it mean to be a poet?" and being given the same answer.

The point is that this question needs to be posed and pondered daily because the answer, like life, is changing daily. Clinging to yesterday's poem or pat answer, role or rote routine dulls us to the moment's ever-changing aliveness.

True, what this "ever-changing aliveness" presents us with in any given moment can be lackluster and, yes, prosaic. Whether you are a monk in a monastery or a poet in the world, there are meals to prepare, bills to pay, and laundry to do. Expanding your awareness to perceive the extraordinary concealed in the ordinary, the Divine hidden in the mundane, and the poem pulsing within the prose is, essentially, a poetic task shared by monk and poet alike.

The monastic vows (which are ideally meant to facilitate this awareness in the monk) are also at work in the poet, albeit in a less formalized, structured way. Receptivity to the muse also requires a certain poverty of spirit; an obedience to whatever form the moment takes; a stable attentiveness to wherever you're standing; and even a chastity that could be defined as a simple, pure, and unencumbered way of seeing, being, and listening that draws us out of our myopic view of life and the world into the larger and more vibrant Reality.

Ultimately, monk and poet stand the way trees in a forest stand— together, alone.

In a culture conditioned not to listen deeply, they susurrate quietly from the margins, inviting us to step out of the cultural mainstream's arrhythmic pulse, back into the steady beating of our own hearts. A monk does this, first and foremost, through the example of his own life; and, secondly, via a retreat or guesthouse where people from all walks of life can slow down and share in this deep listening.

Poetry can create a similar space where, away from the hubbub and noise, you can be present again—to yourself, life, and the natural world. To yourself *as* life and the natural world. Within this poetic sanctuary, you can rekindle what monks fondly refer to as "a love of the place"—trees, water, hills, earth, sky, and stars—which has shaped centuries of monastic life and this book, subtly, profoundly and, yes, poetically, despite my late abbot's words to the contrary.

— *Daniel Skach-Mills*

Expulsion—1992

Nine Poems After Han Shan

ONE

Even if the tree knew the loggers were coming,
where else could it stand?
Even if the fish knew the pond were being drained,
where else could it swim?
When a valley's flooded, only a fool
wastes time looking for a ford.
When the abbot tells me after compline
you'll be leaving in the morning,
what time is there to pack that much pain?

Two

A monk pushes fruitcake batter into the shape of the pan.
Another trims books to fit the size of the covers.
Stones shape the forest stream.
The forest stream shapes the stones.
You're trying to form rather than be formed
is the reason the abbot gives
when I ask why I'm being told to leave.

THREE

The evening of May fourth, I'm in.
The morning of May fifth, I'm out.
My brown cincture lies on the wardrobe table
like bark from a girdled tree.
My white robe hangs from the closet hook
like the wan ghost of who I was.

Four

The abbot has determined without me
what my return to *secular life* will require;
has cut me a check that,
outside these walls, won't last a week.
Asking him for what I really need,
he cuts me with words that,
inside my heart, I know will slice
through me for years:
a la the Trappist GI Bill of Rights,
you are entitled to nothing.
No closure. No goodbyes.
Only the old monk who stops me
in the hall and whispers:
Don't let them make you bitter.

FIVE

Mist rolls into the hills, blanketing the trees.
Words roll out of the mouth, obscuring the Divine.
Sometimes, nothing in life is clear.
Jade-green water conceals colorful koi.
Dark gray clouds shroud the sun's light.
When religious life casts a shadow,
blinding people to compassion,
I call that: *religious death*.

Six

Five-and-a-half years ago I entered through the front door.
Five-and-a-half years later, I'm leaving through the back.
Gazing into the sky, what do coming and going matter
to migrating geese and thistledown?

SEVEN

On the backs of eastern hills,
sun rises above all our beginnings and endings.
In the apple grove west of the abbey,
yesterday's cloud bank of blossoms
has all but disappeared.
Spring winds don't discriminate
between what stays or goes.
May rains don't choose
which colors get washed away.
Duffel bag in hand, not a wink of sleep,
where do I go from here?
Pain's a broken compass
pointing every direction.
Sorrow's a severed arterial
bleeding all over the map.
This morning, everything's lost
except the orchard's one row
of fallen white petals
turning their own death
into a pathway through the trees.

EIGHT

I'm through following trails.
From now on, let me be like morning glory
feeling its way through this moment's always open gate,
the bird that knows wherever it lands is home.
What could I possibly take from the monastery
that these hills haven't already given me?
The path caked to my boots.
The light and dark side of everything.
Streams running from my eyes.
My walking stick, that has
traveled every pathway
but its own.

NINE

Driving away, the valley's silent.
When the bell rings for noon prayer,
I'll be too far away to hear.
Bell tower, no bell tower,
doesn't love's clarion note
keep right on calling to us?
Turning back once to look,
who, I wonder, will console
the weeping cedars?

IN THIS FOREST OF MONKS—1987-1992

ABBEY ROAD
Trappist Monastery

Life here is single lane.
You can't get around that, or the tractor.
The only rush you'll find here
grows slowly in the ditch.

Pray all you want for direction—
in these parts, the signs (if you can find them)
are as shot through with human holes as God's,
and the closest thing to a traffic signal
is the green light shining through the leaves,
the Red Hills that stop at Dundee.

Right turns, wrong turns,
who can map out or explain
all the bends and curves
that detour a person here—
this life, that requires the same
downshift from overdrive
and turning off the main road
that it always has.

PORTAL

The old monk creaks
like the chapel door he's opening.

The portal his life hinges on
cannot be traversed
over a threshold of words
like *entrance* or *exit*,
open or *closed*,
no matter how hard
prayers push.

Now, everything he touches
is a knob turning into silence.

Stepping through
and beyond himself so many years,
what difference now between inner and outer?
His fingers and the twigs of trees
praying their rosary beads of rain.

Out Of The Trunk

On that side of the tree rain has found,
sunlight leans into what's other
and becomes shine.

Old fir, feeling only the dark cracks,
the two roads it must ascend
outward and upward together,
lets light happen best
circling within its own center;
travels the farthest sheen it knows
standing just where it is.

Walking Before Compline

So what are we
if not these autumn cottonwoods
letting go of everything wind tells them to;
the fences, trespassed by age,
forgiving themselves for the deer?

Tonight,
the abbey pumphouse
splashed with moonlight
is as good a reason as any
to believe in resurrection—
the quiet surge of living water being raised
through rocky layers to the surface.
The moon rising over this
and every narrow valley
into the overarching belief
sky has in everything.

Here, seeking God
is the same dark bend in the road it's always been,
the can't-see-what's-coming curve
that brings finding your way back
to where you really live
down to trusting a movement
that's way over our heads:
love, mapless as an owl.
The bell like a star
I can hear.

SYNESTHESIA

The monastery bell tinges twilight
with the zested pitch of citron,
its tart reverb tingling my nose
with a rind's ringing scent.

Like stitch, like weave,
this note is the bell's metallic thread
brocading my flesh with timbre,
a sonorous sharp penetrating
the fir-needled pincushions of hills.

Within each pupil's ring of sight,
this peal is the feather-soft arrowhead
of southbound geese
piercing the sky's purple bruise of cloud—
its downpour of sound:
a tarnished weary silver.

On my tongue,
the tone resonates tea
tolling from an ancient bush
in the mountains
no one has ever found.

Watching An Old Trappist Drink Tea

There is no drinker.
That shallow cup was emptied
years ago.

Nothing to hold on to now
but the rough hand-thrown mug
cradled precariously as prayer
between the crumbling clay of his palms,
the vessel that begins empty and ends empty
no matter how fast or slow he sips.

Bitterness, weakness,
sweetness when it happens
is just the vow he's steeped in,
his parting lips kissed
by the passing steam
of whatever life pours out,
the fragile handle he knows
we have on things
as chipped and cracked
as it ever was.

ON RETREAT

Sun rising through the monastery window.
A single ray needling light through a thousand pines.
Before morning clears these fog-blanketed hills,
monks will be soughing lauds.

On my desk,
the mug of tea is as cold as my pen.
The sheet of paper's blank.
Prayer, in these matters, doesn't help.
Poems arise, or they don't.

Wind blows through the trees at will,
but who can quote it,
or its source?

A Forest's Theory Of Human Evolution

No, not from primates,
but from the longstanding desire
of trees who yearned to move—
oak and beech, hickory and fir
evolving into what we call
this body's trunk, limbs,
the ten grounded taproots of the toes,
twigs of fingers.

Even terms like *branching out*,
cutting me down,
or the gnarled old,
bent as weeping cedars,
all point to a stump's concentric circles
whorled onto the pad at each finger's end,
the veined foliage of our hands
leafing out to caress sky,
birds landing,
your catkin kin.

WINGSPAN

Beak poised like a warrior's feather-adorned spear,
the heron is back, perched again
on the flat tarred roof overlooking
the cloister garth
and the pond.

And now,
landing as if from out of nowhere,
Father John Baptist is up there too,
another old bird—flightless,
except for prayer—
waving his arms *shoo shoo*,
the long white sleeves of his cowl
flapping like woolen wings at the Great Blue
whose coverts extend to him nothing less
than this open invitation to heaven's
borderless wingspan.
Who hasn't a clue that he's
just one more bird of appetite,
another stab of hunger
this monk—vowed to
the belly's molt—has been
putting to flight
for years.

HERONS

It's their longstanding pact with mud
that impresses me, this ancient covenant they have
with what oozes up from beneath the surface:
reeds and sedges shoring up the legs,
underpinning the toes.

How they remain unflappable
in the fetid fen of whatever happens
waiting for what nourishes—
there must be something holy in this:
the pointed truth of the beak
shattering again and again
the shallow hunger of its own reflection,
filtering out of the stillness
those movements it needs
to live.

BOWING TO BIRDS
After Tom Crawford

Juncos,
I bow this morning
not to these fallen feathers
of snow I'm shoveling
but to you
the most Cistercian of birds
your black-hooded flock
pecking at the branches
of the apple tree
in such numbers
I lose track of you
the way I sometimes
lose track of myself
in the church after dark
when I'm alone
and what can't be seen
is all there is
to feed on.

A CHRISTMAS CANDLING

Tonight
window-ledged
one fragile-winged flame
flutters toward a world moth-hungry for light.

Tonight, here, what difference could it make?
One child-candle kindling to warm,
mere straw in the wind
firing the wick in the storm
that for an instant
makes the whole world
seem suddenly
stable.

UNDER THE TREE
Trappist Abbey—1991

This Christmas Eve, let's not get over-involved in too much decorating.
Let's notice what's simple—like the first smell of Douglas Fir wafting
through the house.
                    — Father John Baptist Hasbrouck, OCSO

Bring the stars in.
Let a tree's needle-stitched skirt
conifer-clothe the room.

Lying prone on the floor,
the fir's hardwood cousin,
become small again.
Slip beneath this ribboned
ruffle of boughs
into the gift the world is.

Be one of them,
bright and rapt
and waiting.

Live inside *that*:
the space between root and star,
a secret and its telling.

Hiking The Hill That Overlooks The Trappist Abbey Prior To First Vespers of Christmas, 1990

My breath pluming white into December
could, to God, be incense rising out
of the puffing thurible of my body.
Up here, it's impossible to tell for the fog
where breathing ends and the Divine begins,
or just what the larger picture is supposed to be
fifty feet beyond the farm's broken fence,
or the crow disappearing like ash
off the corbel of the smoking chimney.
Yes, I'm here, vowed to the landscape
and what I know is there, but can't see
any more than the next person.
So what is Christmas, anyway,
if not this empty barn, the once carefully baled
straw of our lives scattered and waiting,
star-starved for a nativity?
Today, the feel of snow in the air
—here, but not yet— is also a matter of faith,
as is the spire-wick'd candle
of the monastery bell tower
hidden from view by a wreath of fir;
trees that, by vespers, will all be Cistercian—
the white cowl of fresh snow pulled silently
over the evergreen vow of their stability.

In This Forest Of Monks

What we love is what we grow to resemble.

— St. Bernard of Clairvaux

supple is good—
the prayer bending low to the ground
like snow-robed boughs,
the rustling leaves: what you hope to become,
moved more and more by what's invisible.

Beneath this hood of conifer shade,
what deeper profession to silence could you make
than the deer moving you to sudden
and broader leaps of faith,
the moss clinging, stone-stubborn,
to the belief that stillness matters?

Ear pressed a lifetime
to psalmodies of cedar, antiphons of oak,
what older organum could you hope to hear
than the halved choir of your own heart
steadily chanting evergreen
in a world that's deciduous?
Silence not saying anything
trees don't already know.

ICON

Pray to this morning doe—
her eyes: two radiant black madonnas
bestowing grace from bramble

on the trail below the hermitage;
her body: a sanctuary of expectant stillness
that clearly wasn't anticipating the prickly thorn of me—

a young monk scavenging,
gathering, like her, these silent morsels of daybreak
onto the animal hunger of the tongue.

What icon, holy as it is, can compare
with the rapt gaze of this?—
the dawn-lit vigil lamps of our faces

burning, one before the other;
mist rising like incense as she slips,
a white-robed tail vanishing,

quiet as a chapel, into these deeper vows
she's made to copse and canebrake,
shinleaf and salal,

the wild apple of her heart beating
toward the hidden cloisters of owls,
the secret shrines they tuck, chanting, into the trees.

GARNISHMINT

A patch of mint.
A patch of mint growing
beside the footbridge.

Today I mowed over the mint.
No one else was there
so I lingered a while,
a sprig or two longer
so as not to be cut off from
that shimmery-scented buzz,
that shaken bell tingling the air.

Tonight, a patch of mint.
Tonight a patch of mint
growing on my shoes.
Mint oil on my shoes
so that every step
garnishes the world.

Tonight my shoes
are footbridges for mint.

Ivy

Photosynthesis at its most ravenous,
you've consumed the arbor vitae,
devoured the fence.

Now, where the gate once stood,
your hinged jaw swings open like a snake's
letting in what's left of the yard.

Little wonder gardeners the world over
pitchfork and burn you, condemn you with invectives
like *Devil's Root* and *Satan's Tongue*.

Slithering around fruit tree and conifer,
you beguile us as a start
into believing you could be Eden;

that your shining scales,
weighted naturally toward the light,
are tipped in our favor.

GARDENER

It's all prayer—
and that includes the vetch and purslane,
chickweed and quack grass that brother Joseph,
eighty-years young, is bowing to,
hoe in hand in the field beside the abbey,
the trailing litanies of summer squash
and eggplant, purple as Lent,
bringing him down onto
the crusty red beets of his knees
poking through ripped jeans,
fruit-laden limbs raising him up
on legs bowed like cucumbers.

In church, out of church,
what difference does it make?
Gospel and pruning guide both showing him
how to cut everything back.
The kneeling that's required
whether he's planting starts or prayers.
Death, that's composted down
to nothing more now
than the thin peel of his skin
being covered with earth,
same as it was in life.
The withering stalk of his body
going to seed like
it always has.

No Fear

At one with what is,
a dying monk knows
there isn't anything wrong with him.

He isn't sick
any more than a woman giving birth is sick.
He doesn't struggle to survive at all costs
any more than snow struggles
to keep from melting in the sun.

Like the gourd decaying in his garden,
he knows the center of everything
is emptiness.

Unlike other men,
he isn't afraid
to let what looks like nothing
appear as himself.

Trappist Burial

Don't ask why we pull the cowl's white hood
down over the wrinkled rind of the face.
Wasn't this monk vowed to more
than what can be perceived through
the now sight-pitted fruit of his eyes,
the fleshy peel of his senses?

Don't ask why there's no wooden box.
Isn't mystery always ripe with more
than what we can squeeze comfortably inside a box?
Our orchard of core questions, all sown in Eden,
about what to do with what's fallen,
why everything we love gets trimmed back
continually to the root.

When Father Felix died,
we planted him next to the church,
under the dying apricot tree.

By next summer, well, what can I tell you?
Isn't true abundance always weighed
on a broader scale than just avoiding bruises,
picking and choosing from this harvest
we call a life?

More like resurrection, really,
the living reaching up,
taking into their hands what's freely given—
the crop appearing that year
from decaying limbs,
the largest anyone had seen.

WHAT REMAINS

A dead monk leaves behind little—
days, strung together like prayer beads,
have slipped through his fingers.
Nights he burned like a vigil candle
through the darkness
have all melted away.

Even the three religious medals
found in his drawer—so old no one could tell
who the holy personages are—
resemble the life here:
worn faces you pass,
day after day
in the hallway.
Saints you don't
even recognize.

MONKS

Here, when one of the brothers says,
We have so much in common
it means something—
like the army surplus blankets
shot through with holiness
by the silent artillery of moths.
The monk in the choir stall behind you
sucking the flat white whole notes of his teeth,
thirty-two years, through the Salve
and the Amen.

Chanting lauds this morning,
shouldn't daybreak dawn on all of us
as the one more chance that it is
to try and sustain the harmony,
the common voice we're all longing to hear
rising out of the dark?

Morning after morning,
it's what they're all seeking
to become, these old monks:
sunlight quietly entering,
then leaving the room;
embracing and letting go
of everything,
all at once.

A Poem After Tseng Chi

Purple vetch twining through the cloister fence.
Where the streambed lies parched of all direction,
we take Saint Aelred's trail.
A fallen fir becomes our footbridge.
Thistledown high in a web becomes our north star.
Beneath this dusk-hushed canopy of green,
how easily we forget to follow our usual compass of words,
the narrow pathways of our tongues
wandering silently off every topic into trees.

CLEAR-CUT
Trappist Abbey—1989

A shade where shade was.
A swath where the word *saw*
cannot see eye-to-eye on anything
but the past tense
with its identical rip-toothed twin.

Kneeling where rain has wept torrents
down this hillside's stubbled cheek,
yours is the fallen world I pray for—
my tongue as stumped for reasons
as this fir's speechless heart,
the tree's silent rootedness
that could not move anywhere
but to and from its own center,
awareness expanding,
year after year,
into this outer ring's
final soundless toll,
time's invisible bleed.

What I Don't Point Out To The Old Monk Who's Planting Poplars With Me In The Mud Beside The Swale

The owl preening its silky cravat of feathers
on a branch above our heads.
Trillium blooming white boutonnieres
out of the creek's muddy lapels.
The shrew tucking itself into the cottonwood's
velvet cummerbund of moss.

Note, as well, how mum I am about the muskrat,
how hushed concerning the horned lark.
The way I draw no attention to this poplar shaft
I (a so-called celibate) am thrusting
deep into the field's wet waiting,
the landscape vowed only
to this love affair it's having with life,
rather than dreams, coming true.

Ankle-deep in mud,
why trudge on about the obvious
to a monk who's spent years
slogging through darkness,
our boots sinking like roots into a world
more out of sight than in?
The skunk cabbage rising now
like a yellow flame out of the soil,
earth's dark lamp growing us
as silently as light
into God.

Hermit
For Father Mark

On the hill behind the abbey
woods claim you, a tree among trees
living together, alone.

In your hermitage aspersed
with pine resin, seeds from bracts of cones,
what else could prayer be but tinder?
The duff of words igniting
then dying down
until only their mute heat remains.
The fire in your belly stoked
with humanity's burning log
of ashes-to-ashes, dust-to-dust sorrows
unfurling their tattered pennant
from the mast of your care-charred stove pipe,
your white flag of personal surrender
smoking God out, forty-plus years,
teary-eyed into the open.

Love and woodcutting,
meditation and oak,
for you it's all the same—
pine being just one more way
that passion fells us,
the curved ax blade of your smile
slicing past what's surface,
splitting open the heart.
The solitary stacking of days
you spend working with what sticks

to the flesh: slivers, pitch.
The patient curing before
becoming flame.

FLAME

Heart cloistered in tinted glass,
this sanctuary candle beats
the ruby-red of a hummingbird's throat,
its undulating pulse a fire in the breast,
all flicker and dart,
the flame's iridescent feather
flashing a glimpse of what's here
(but rarely seen)
into the corner of faith's
slow-to-see eye.

Ablaze at the tip,
this taper conceals a wick
as prone to fire as the bird's
pistil-whipping tongue,
a snap-match of sun sparked
by a stigma's nectar-beaded glister,
the flower's pollen-blazing anther.

Candle suspended, bird hovering,
each over its own altar,
what, I ask you, isn't enlightened here?
The perfect match being
your whole life consumed
by a wing-fanned devotion to flame.
Love, that tears off every
safely closed cover
before striking.

A Monk's Prayer

is small—
thimbleberry barely noticed
near the edge of the trail
pebble glinting at the toe
of your boot
the shape, if it has one,
oval like a hummingbird's egg
born of a conjugal hovering
between heaven and earth,
the open nest of your mouth
giving rise to flights of praise
indistinguishable in size
from that tiny prayer bead of shell
psalms no larger than the tip
of the hatchling's beak
breaking wordlessly
from one world
into another.

WHY MONKS CHOOSE SILENCE

To step out forever
from under the sagging
syllable-shingled roof
of the mouth.

To be the vast
unfeathered nest of emptiness
out of which sound arises,
and into which it lands.

To live like a furrow
listening inwardly to a seed—
love's infant hand
knocking from inside,
wanting in to be the world.

Refectory Prayer

1

This is the place of hunger
for what can and cannot be seen.
Hunger in the belly, hunger in the soul,
this is where the ravenous cave
of the human mouth opens
into its own emptiness;
where all your tongue has to lick
is its own craving for everything
but silence.

2

In times past,
a monk late to table
would circle the refectory
begging food from his brothers.
Wooden bowl
wooden utensils
wooden rules.

3

The noon meal begins with a prayer;
ends, as it always does,
with the leftover dollop of faith
in what remains:
wilted broccoli
day-old lima beans
this life, that's a set menu.

4

We eat in silence
while a book's read aloud.
We eat silence
until the empty space
between the words
is all that's left on our plates.

5

Every Thursday: burritos.
This sameness we chew
until we can taste
what's hidden inside.

6

Ladle it or not,
you can't help but taste
the soup of community here—
everything from the charred leftovers
of Our Lady of the Valley on
mixed together daily
and served up out of the pot.

Now, when I press my lips to a cup, a spoon,
I'm kissing everything that's gone before;
the dead, too, who still nourish us
just as surely as this silent community
of mugs and bowls they ate and drank from,
earthenware broken and repaired so many times
who can say what's holding it, or any of us, in place—
the lifelong helping of prayer, perhaps,
pressed into the fissures and cracks,
the deep bond of it, invisible as glue
that holds together quietly,
but is there.

How To Make A Monastery Fruitcake
In Memory Of Brother Eugene, Fruitcake Bakery Manager

For a dark cake, begin before dawn.
Check your supply of emptiness,
the most important ingredient—
empty sink and oven, cake boxes and pans,
the giant steel mixing bowl Lao-tzu would have loved
precisely because of what it doesn't contain.

Intone flour, cinnamon, nutmeg, cloves.
Pray a prayer the shape of pecan.
Blend, until all the separate ingredients
become a community that holds together.
Don't confuse who you are
and the Order you've taken vows to
with the order that you're filling.

Stir from this center of stillness
twenty-seven years,
until the hunger to measure success
is satiated by the question:
*so how many fruitcakes does
the world really need?*

Set the timer of your life
to a pace slow enough
for the answer to bake, cool,
be dipped in brandy and aged.

One. Just this one.

THE MONK WHO BAKES BREAD

no longer believes in the measure-for-measure God
of the recipe books,
has little faith, if any, in the predestined endings
set forth by timers,
the finely sifted claims to inerrancy held
by cups and spoons.

Blended to life,
call his a leavened devotion to resurrection
appearing from within each cracked tomb of grain,
the hunger that presses his hands,
dawn after dawn,
deep into the just-risen flesh.

Cowl white as the flour he scoops, mixes,
forms *pat pat* into loaves shaped like naves,
it is his chest, filled with the invisible yeast of breath,
that knows by heart the patient
kneading together of days,
how long love takes to rise.

RETURN—2011-2012

RECALLING THE MONASTERY
After Han Shan

When snow fell this winter
I thought about my brothers.
When leaves unfurled this spring
I remembered the Red Hills.
Shaded trails wandered into a thousand hidden places.
Sunlit rills trickled through an open grove.
Alas, although nearly twenty years have passed,
recalling the monastery hurts.

Flag

For years, I rose before dawn in still woods,
retired to ringing bells.
Strange, in this life, how nothing lasts like loss.
Inside, I'm still a monk. My heart is in the Red Hills.
Indian plum and snowberry grow there,
if you know where to look,
and wild flag, this time of year,
paints the forest purple.

RETURN

The monastery church is silent. No one knows I'm here.
Nineteen years ago I was told to leave this place.
Unlike people, birds flying over these sunset-red hills
don't try to perch on shadows.

THROUGH THE CLOISTER FENCE

Many of the monks I knew here are dead.
The trees I planted are green.

Which ones, or how many, who can say?

Peering through the cloister fence,
I cry trying to count the cemetery crosses
that have sprouted since I left.

WHAT I, THE LANDSCAPE, OFFER AS HEALING WHEN YOU RETURN TO VISIT THE ABBEY NINETEEN YEARS AFTER BEING EXPELLED

The pine, like Zen, not knowing it's pine.
The pond giving anything that wants to
a place to reflect.

Across the valley of nineteen years
I graft you again to snag and nurse log,
a wooded path professed to whatever's fallen.
Hemmed by spruce and fir needle
I vest you in this grove's white robe of sunlight,
a forest's ancient Order of ravel and weave,
the bell's fraying echo.

Thrumming beneath the white oaks,
what truer enclosure could my crimson meadow offer
than this clover-crooned cenobium's
humming hive of cells,
its cloistered embroidery of sound
stitching you back to hiddenness,
mending what was cut away
with the invisible thread
of love for a place
that a bee's flight is.

How A Bell Can Pull You

Sighing firs echo my longing.
Flowing streams reflect my tears.
The vespers bell fades, as it always does,
like sunlight through the trees,
but the hand pulling the bell-rope
is no longer mine.

What I Follow Into The Red Hills

Shadows erasing the blue-green hillsides.
Nothing ahead of me clear.
On a cool evening breeze:
the sweet smell of timothy.
In my aging hand: the walking stick
a monk gave me over twenty years ago.
Eschewing trails thick with pine guff,
crossing streams padded with moss,
it seems to know the way.
If it's leading me to the tree it came from,
I wouldn't even know it.

Ash

In Memory Of Brother Michael Farrelly, OCSO

Long before I would feel in my own clear-cut cloistered life
a razed tree's strange and sudden displacement—
the heart's unseen taproot still anchored deeply in a place,
the trunk and limbs stripped away, gone—
you gave me this walking stick hewn from ash ...
you, who surfaced as your mother drowned
beneath the breaking waters of childbirth;
who crossed the dark and roiling sea from Ireland;
later, cut loose your moorings from a marriage.
Who passed on to me one blazing autumn
this token of the severed world
you knew still walked beside you,
supporting, sometimes leading
like a companion or a friend.

Had I been at your funeral I would have bent down,
my spine curved like a winter-weighted branch
to kiss your two clubbed feet;
bowed to all the comings and goings,
the myriad twists and turns of love—
leafed out and lopped—that grew out of,
and so resembled, their beautifully gnarled roots.
How they lifted you like these treetops
from earth toward sky,
this view I have, climbing upward,
that could be the valley of your smile
still stretched out before me
between the red hills of your cheeks.

You who placed ash into my hand—
tree named for what remains
after everything's burned away—
knowing it was us.

PAUSING WHERE THE CLIMB TURNS STEEPER

Wandering these woods without map or compass,
uncertain of direction as a monk lost in prayer,
I pause where the climb turns steeper
to watch and listen.

Overhead, birds darting in and out of leaves
don't reveal where they're heading.
At my feet, sounds scurry out from under
the circling hawk of every word.
This hill I'm standing on speaks up silently,
the way it has for centuries.
Twenty years flown are but a flutter
through these trees.

In Woods East Of The Abbey

I stitch a robe from dusk's mottled pelt.
In a grove of sapling alder
I plait a hymnal of birdcalls,
a psalter of rustling leaves.

From the cherry-pitted scat
of ambling night coons
I daub a shrine to the insatiable bowel
of whatever happens.

You who long to be forgiven of trails,
absolved of wanting only what comes at the end,
see how I keep this vigil for you
to Oregon ash and dewberry,
hazelnut and pine;
how I invoke the sun's red
aureole of flame
circling the towhee's eye
on your behalf.

In these hills,
prayer is the sleek slip and vanish of fur
getting down on all fours,
light's silent shadow lining
the dark pool of your mouth
with stones from the forest streambed,
the pointed frond of your tongue
lapping at spoor awash in autumn rain—
your lips wet with the kiss of what

lives beneath the surface,
the silt of what it tastes like
to follow yourself home.

MANZOU

Abandoning trails east of the abbey, I head into dusky woods.
Cicada's trill marks a turn. A shaft of setting sunlight
arrows where to stop and notice the pine.
Deer slip silently into the bracken.
The bell fades quietly into the trees.
Unless you've paced your life to manzou,
you won't understand my walking stick
beating me again to the shrine on the hill.

In This Cleavage Of Leaves
At The Shrine To Our Lady Of Guadalupe
Trappist Abbey

At the base of your hilltop shrine,
at the foot of your image draped beneath
a lichen-laced mantilla of fir and oak:
two half-circles of piled stones;
two cupped crescents joined
to form a woman's breasts.

Certainly no monk's doing,
this basalt bosom trimmed
by a mossy flounce I kneel to touch,
loose a stone the way one might pull
a ribbon from a bodice.

In your cleavage powdered with pine pollen,
flushed by autumn's heartbeat
of crimson cordate leaves
I rest my head,
let the loss fall like rain
into this vale of tears.

Where a pointed sandstone pap protrudes,
dusk lactates its milky white light,
faithful as a goddess.

HILL MOTHER
*After Paulann Petersen's "Song For One Who Waits
In The Forest"*

Lady in the Red Hills,
I come bearing a porcelain bowl etched with plum blossoms,
dried tea wrapped in a crinkle of handmade paper,
its rolling folds white as virgin snow.

Lady who watches from sun-tinged fir,
I met you in summer beneath a veil of blue sky,
its azure weave trailing into a stream's flowing hem,
low-flying swallows tatting a grassy swath
of Queen Anne's lace.

I came to you years ago,
a young monk offering green poems on scrap paper,
verses I braceleted with jute around your delicate
vine-maple wrists, my eyes unable to meet
the leaf-lidded sunbursts of your gaze.

Hill mother, all my windbreaks have fallen.
Branches I'll never touch are soughing out of reach.
When I am too old to hear them,
you must use your mantle
to gather me into their sound.

GLOSSARY/NOTES

Abbey Road: the monastery is located on Abbey Road.

Across the valley of nineteen years: Cistercian/Trappist monasteries are typically built in valleys or low lying areas. This distinguishes them from Benedictine houses which are usually built on rises or hilltops.

Bell-rope: the abbey bell is rung by hand to call the monks to prayer. I was the bell-ringer for approximately three years.

Cenobium: from the Latin *coenobium*, convent, and from the Greek, *koinobion*, or life in community. Cenobites are monks or nuns who live in common in a monastery or convent.

Cincture: the brown leather belt worn around the outside of the monastic robe.

Cistercian *see:* Trappist.

Clear-cut: in 1989, many of the monks were surprised and angry to discover that the abbey had clear-cut and sold five acres of timber adjacent to the monastery picnic grounds.

Compline: the final common monastic prayer of the day, usually completed by 8 PM.

Cowl: the hooded white choir robe worn by Cistercian/Trappist monks.

Desert Fathers: the first Christian hermits who fled to the deserts of Egypt, Arabia, Persia, and Palestine when Christianity became the official religion of the Roman Empire in the fourth century A.D.

Dundee: the town of Dundee, Oregon.

Flag: a small iris.

Halved choir: monastery choirs are split in half, with the monks facing one another as they chant the psalms.

Han Shan: a Chinese Taoist/Buddhist recluse who lived in the 9th century in Chekiang province, at the base of Han Yen, or "Cold Cliff," a two-day walk from the East China Sea. Han Shan's work reveals a disgruntlement with the prevailing cultural, religious, and political system of his day. This could be due, in part, to his being rejected, time and again, for an imperial post by the Board of Personnel due to some physical defect. I chose Han Shan's poetic style to convey my monastic experience of rejection and pain.

Lady in the Red Hills: "Lady" refers to Our Lady of Guadalupe, the patroness after whom the abbey is named. The abbey is located in the Red Hills of Dundee, Oregon.

Lao-tzu: the Taoist sage who is reputed to have written the *Tao Te Ching*, or the *Book of the Virtue of the Way* in China in the 6th century BC. Referring to the empty mixing bowl, chapter 11 of the *Tao Te Ching* reads: "We shape clay into a bowl, but it is the bowl's emptiness that makes it useful."

Lauds: morning prayer, sung in common by the monks, usually around 6:30 AM.

Lent: in the Roman Catholic tradition, purple is the liturgical color for the season of Lent.

Manzou: a Chinese farewell that means "go slowly."

Nave(s): the long central hall of a church.

OCSO: stands for: Order of Cistercians of the Strict Observance (*see:* Trappist/Cistercian).

Organum: a form of polyphonic chant in which one half of the choir is a tonal step below the other. This creates an unusual and beautiful harmonic variation.

Our Lady of Guadalupe: in Roman Catholicism, the title "Our Lady of Guadalupe" refers to apparitions of Mary at Tepeyac, near Mexico City, in 1531.

Our Lady of the Valley: Our Lady of the Valley Monastery was founded in Valley Falls, Rhode Island by monks from Petit Clairvaux Abbey in Nova Scotia, Canada (est. 1868). Prior to being destroyed by fire in 1950, monks from Our Lady of the Valley established St. Joseph's Abbey in Spencer, Massachusetts; and, in 1948, Spencer monks founded Our Lady of Guadalupe Abbey in Pecos, New Mexico. The Pecos location did not work out, and the monks moved to Oregon in 1955.

Professed to whatever's fallen: monks first make simple, and then solemn profession (or vows) to the monastic life. Simple profession usually lasts three years, after which a solemn profession is made for life.

Saint Aelred's Trail: a trail on the monastery property. Saint Aelred was the third Cistercian abbot (1147-1167) of Rievaulx Abbey in Yorkshire, England.

Salve: (pronounced "saul-vey") the Salve Regina, a hymn to Mary typically sung at the end of compline.

Sanctuary candle: in Roman Catholicism, the Eucharist (or Blessed Sacrament) is housed within a tabernacle inside the church. The sanctuary candle burns continuously, symbolizing Christ's presence.

Shrine: the shrine to Our Lady of Guadalupe, located atop the hill on the monastery property.

Synesthesia: a momentary exchange or fusion of the senses. A common phenomenon in Taoism (especially when reading or writing Taoist poetry), and in some schools of Buddhism.

Thurible: a censer on a long chain, often used in processionals, that is swung back and forth.

Trappist/Cistercian: the Cistercians began as a reform of the Benedictine monastic Order in Dijon, France in 1098. The first Cistercian monastery was called *Cistertium*. In modern French it is called *Cîteaux*. A later and much stricter reform of the Cistercian Order in the 17th century at the abbey of La Trappe in Normandy was adopted by many of the Cistercian houses. The nickname "Trappist" comes from this reform.

Trims books: the abbey industries included a bookbindery and a fruitcake bakery.

Tseng Chi: a Chinese poet (1084-1166) born in Kanchou. My poem was inspired by his poem, *On The Sanchu Road*, in which he writes: "where the river turns shallow I take the trail/the canopy of green remains forever shady."

Vale of tears: these words are from the Salve Regina, a hymn to Mary sung at the end of compline. The line is, "Have pity on us, poor banished children of Eve, mourning and weeping in this vale of tears."

Vespers: evening prayer chanted in common by the monks anywhere between 5 and 6 PM.

Wardrobe: the monks' clothing was held in a common wardrobe. This room also included a tailor shop and a laundry.

You're trying to form rather than be formed: as a junior monk, not yet solemnly vowed, I was considered to be "in formation." During this time, I began to see how decisions that impacted the community were being made with little or no group dialog (*see:* Clear-cut). Expressing my feelings and advocating for a community forum was, I assume, what prompted the answer I received.

ABOUT THE AUTHOR

Daniel Skach-Mills was born in Coeur d'Alene, Idaho, and raised in Portland, Oregon. He holds an undergraduate degree from Marylhurst University, Marylhurst, Oregon; and a graduate degree in counseling psychology from St. Martin's University in Lacey, Washington.

His award-winning poetry has been published in a variety of publications and anthologies, including: *The Christian Science Monitor; Open Spaces; The Christian Century; The Journal of Daoist Philosophy and Practice;* and *Prayers To Protest: Poems That Center And Bless Us* (Pudding House Publications, 1998). His chapbook, *Gold: Daniel Skach-Mills's Greatest Hits, 1990-2000* was published by Pudding House in 2001; *The Tao of Now,* (Ken Arnold Books, 2008) was listed as one of the "150 outstanding Oregon poetry books" by Jeff Baker, columnist for *The Oregonian*; David Biespiel, editor of *Poetry Northwest;* and Jim Scheppke, Oregon State Librarian; and *The Hut Beneath the Pine: Tea Poems* (2011) was a finalist for the 2012 Oregon Book Award.

Daniel has been a featured reader in the northwest at Barnes and Noble (Vancouver, WA); Blackbird Wine Bar; Broadway Books; Eastrose Unitarian Fellowship; First Unitarian Church; The Hundredth Monkey Art Studio; KBOO Radio; Lan Su Chinese Garden; Living Earth Gatherings; Looking Glass Bookstore; Marylhurst University; Moonstruck Chocolate Café; Nritya Mandala Mahavihara Newari Buddhist Temple; Our House of Portland; The Q Center; Rilassi Coffee House; The Tenth Muse Books (Seaside); The Milwaukie Poetry Series; Oregon Literary Arts; and The Friends of William Stafford.

A volunteer docent for Lan Su Chinese Garden since 2005, he currently lives with his partner in Portland, Oregon.